THE ROYAL COURT THEATRE, AMBASSADOR THEATRE
GROUP, GUY CHAPMAN AND MARK GOUCHER
with the assistance of the Austrian Cultural Institute present:

HOLY MOTHERS

by Werner Schwab

in a new English version by Meredith Oakes

First British performance at the New Ambassadors Theatre
West Street, London WC2 on 27th May 1999

Presented by:

Royal Court Theatre
St Martins Lane, WC2N 4BG
Tel: 0171 565 5000 Fax: 0171 565 5001

Ambassadors Theatre Group
25 Shaftesbury Avenue, W1V 7HA
Tel: 0171 494 0333 Fax: 0171 494 0034

Guy Chapman Associates
1-2 Henrietta Street, WC2E 8PS
Tel: 0171 379 7474 Fax: 0171 379 8484

Mark Goucher
35-39 Old Street, EC1
Tel: 0171 439 1589 Fax: 0171 439 1590

Holy Mothers is produced through special arrangement with Eva
Feitzinger, Thomas Sessler Verlag, Johannesgrasse 12, A-1010 Vienna,
Austria.

Copyright agent for the original work: Thomas Sessler Verlag,
Johannesgasse 12, A-1010 Vienna, Austria.

Copyright agent for English translation: Casarotto Ramsay Ltd,
60-66 Wardour Street, London, W1V 4ND. All rights and enquiries
concerning this English language version should be made in the first
instance to Casarotto Ramsay Ltd.
Tel 0171 287 4450, Fax 0171 287 9128

Holy Mothers

by Werner Schwab

in a new English version by Meredith Oakes

Cast in order of appearance

Erna Valerie Lilley
Grete Paola Dionisotti
Mariedl Linda Dobell

with Stephanie Bagshaw, Patricia Valentine and Kelly Wright

Director Richard Jones
Designer Stewart Laing
Lighting Designer Pat Collins
Sound Designer Gareth Fry
Fight Director Alison De Burgh
Casting Lisa Makin and Julia Horan
Assistant Director Kitty Malone
Production Manager Jon Howes
Company Stage Manager Rob Young
Deputy Stage Manager Julie Issott
Set Construction Scenery Jessel
Painted by John Campbell, Scenic Studios
Costume Supervisor Heather Leat
Production Photography Manuel Harlan
Press Peter Thompson Associates

The producers would like to thank the following for their help with this production: Wardrobe care by Lever Brothers. Thanks to Ben Tranchell, Francis Alexander, Lisa Popham and Fiona Carpernter at DeWynters.

THE COMPANY

Werner Schwab (writer)
Holy Mothers (Die Präsidentinnen) (première: Münchner Kammerspiele);
Übergewicht, Unwichtig: Unform (première: Schauspielhaus Wien); Mein Hundemund
(première: Schauspielhaus Wien); Offene Gruben, Offene Fenster, Ein Fall (première:
Studiozelt. Donaufestival); Mesalliance (première: Schauspielhaus Graz); Der Himmel,
Mein Lieb, Meine Sterbende Beute (première Staatstheater Stuttgart); Endlich Tot,
Endlich Keine Luft Mehr (première: Saarbrüken); Pornogeographie (première:
Schauspeielhaus Graz/Steirischer Herbst); Faust: Mein Brustkorb: Mein Helm
(première: Potsdam); Der Reizende Reigen nach dem Reigen des Reizenden Herrn
Arthur Schnitzler (première: Schauspielhaus Zürich); Eskalation (première
Schauspeilhaus Hamberg, Malersaal); Antiklima(x) (première: Kampnagel Fabrik,
Hamburg).

Meredith Oakes (translator)
As a translator: Die Prasidentinnen (Holy Mothers) by Werner Schwab, Kabale und
Liebe by Schiller, Miss Julie by Strindberg, Italian Night by Horvath, Elizabeth II by
Bernhard, The New Menoza by Lenz, Princesses by Fatima Gallaire.
As an author: Faith (Royal Court Theatre); The Editing Process (Royal Court
Theatre); Mind the Gap (Hampstead Theatre); The Neighbour (RNT).
Librettos include: The Triumph of Berauty and Deceit (Channel 4); Jump into my Sack
(Mecklenburg Opera); Chemistry (ENO).
Television includes: Prime Suspect (as co-writer).
Radio includes: Glide.

Pat Collins (lighting designer)
Theatre includes: Once Upon a Mattress (Lincoln Centre at the Cort); An American
Daughter (Lincoln Center at the Plymouth); A Delicate Balance, The Sisters
Rosensweig, Conversations With My Father, The Heidi Chronicles, I'm Not
Rappaport, Execution of Justice, Arsenic and Old Lace, Sherlock's Last Case, Ain't
Misbehavin', Baby, Steaming, Stages, King of Hearts (Lincoln Theater Theater); Death
and The Kings Horseman, The Three Penny Opera (Vivien Beaumont);The Floating
Lightbulb (Vivien Beaumont); Measure for Measure (Mitzi E. Newhouse); Ain't
Misbehavin' (Her Majesty's); The Illusion (Old Vic); Into the Woods (Royal).
Opera includes: Barber of Seville (Royal Opera at the Shaftesbury); Katya Kabanova,
The Ring Cycle (Royal Opera); Rienze, Mazeppa, Simon Boccanegra, The Plumber's
Gift (ENO); La Incoronazione di Poppea (WNO).
Ballet includes: Sleeping Beauty (Royal Ballet).
Awards include: Tony Award (I'm Not Rappaport, Lincoln Center); Drama Desk
Award (Execution of Justice, Lincoln Center); Tony Nomination (The Three Penny
Opera, Vivian Beaumont).

Paola Dionisotti
Theatre includes: Genesis, Mary, Mary (Freehold); Seven Deadly Sins, A Streetcar
Named Desire (Citizens); The Trial (London Theatre Group), 'Tis Pity She's a
Whore, Way of the World, Knots (Actors Company); Commitments (Bush Theatre);
King Lear (Young Vic); Can't Pay, Won't Pay (Criterion); The Fourth Wall (Drill
Hall); Crime and Punishment (Lyric Hammersmith); The White Devil, The Way of the
World, Mary Stuart (Greenwich Theatre); The Wandering Jew, Countrymania,
Square Rounds, Richard II, The Machine Wreckers (NT); On the Verge (Sadler's
Wells); Ghosts (Edinburgh Lyceum); Britannicus (Crucible, Sheffield); Vassa, The
Trojan Women (Gate, London); The Iceman Cometh, Pillars of the Community, The
Taming of the Shrew, Measure for Measure, Antony and Cleopatra, Moscow Gold,
Sore Throats, Heresies (RSC); Peer Gynt (World Tour); Plays by Gertrude Stein
(Citizens Theatre); The Misfits (Royal Exchange); Office Suite (West Yorkshire
Playhouse), Camino Real (RSC).
Television includes: Commitments, Baal, Fame is the Spur, The Killing Time, The
Gentle Touch, A Fine Romance, The Young Ones, A Murder is Announced, The Bill,
They Never Do What You Want, The Monocled Mutineer, Drummonds, First

Among Equals, Forever Green, House of Elliot, The Gospels, Just William, Devil's Advocate, Peak Practice, Harbour Lights.
Film includes: The Sailor's Return, Sakharov, Les Miserables, Vigo: A Passion for Life, The Tichbourne Claimant.

Linda Dobell
Theatre includes: The Good Person of Setzuan, Arabian Nights (Bubble Theatre); Crimson Island, Legends of Evil (Gate); School for Clowns (Lilian Baylis); 4 Mary's, Badenhiem (Second Stride); Slaughterhouse 5, 'Tis Pity She's a Whore, Sarcophagus (Everyman, Liverpool); The Importance of Being Ernest, The Cherry Orchard, The Bald Prima Donna, The Breasts of Tiresias (Crucible, Sheffield); Shagnasty (Union); Lower Depths (Cardboard Citizens); The Miser (RNT).
Television includes: Revolting Women, Scarfe on Sex, A Touch of Frost, Hetty Wainthrop.
Linda is an associate director of the Everyman Liverpool and choreographer for RNT, ROH, Opera North, Scottish Opera, and WNO.

Richard Jones (director)
Theatre includes: Too Clever by Half, A Flea in Her Ear, The Illusion (Old Vic); Le Bourgeois Gentilhomme (RNT); Into the Woods (Phoenix Theatre); La Bete (Broadway / Lyric Hammersmith); Black Snow (American Repertory Theatre); All's Well That Ends Well (Public Theatre, New York); Titanic (Broadway).
Opera includes: The Love for Three Oranges, Die Fledermaus (ENO); Der Fliegende Hollander, Jennfa (Amsterdam); Julius Caesar, The Midsummer Marriage (Munich); Der Ring Des Nibelungen (Royal Opera House); Peulleau et Melisande (Opera North); L'Enfant Les Sortileges, Der Zwerg (Paris); Hansel and Gretal (WNO).
Awards include: Olivier Award (Too Clever by Half, Old Vic); Evening Standard Award (The Illusion, Old Vic); Olivier and Evening Standard Award (Into the Woods, Phoenix Theatre); Openwelt Production of the Year 1994 (Julius Caesar, Munich); Evening Standard Award (Der Ring des Nibelungen, Royal Opera House).

Stewart Laing (designer)
Design work includes productions for Scottish Opera, Opera North, English National Opera, Royal National Theatre, Royal Shakespeare Company, Citizens Company, Almeida and the Royal Court. He has also designed for the West End and Broadway, winning a Tony Award for his work on the musical Titanic.
His work as a director includes: The Homosexual (Tramway); Brainy (CCA); Happy Days (Tramway/Traverse); The Father, The She Wolf, A Long Day's Journey Into Night, Medea (Citizens Company); La Boheme (Scottish Opera Go Round); Cosi Fan Tutte (Scottish Opera); L'heure Espagnole, Breasts of Tiresias (Grange Park Opera).
Future projects include: Myths of the Near Future, based on JG Ballards's science fiction stories. This project is funded by National Lottery New Directions and will be presented at Tramway in Spring 2000.

Valerie Lilley
Theatre includes: Blue Heart (Royal Court and Out of Joint); Flying Blind (Royal Court); Inventing a New Colour (Bristol Old Vic / Royal Court); Killing the Cat (Soho Poly / Royal Court); The Mai, Factory Girls, Once a Catholic, A Love Song for Ulster (Tricycle); Drive On (Lyric, Belfast); Pig's Ear, Breezeblock Park, Shadow of a Gunman (Liverpool Playhouse); Lysistrata (Contact, Manchester); Blood Wedding, My Mother Said I Never Should (Octagon, Bolton); A Madhouse in Goa (Oldham Coliseum); The Cherry Orchard, The Card (New Victoria, Stoke); Jane Eyre (Crucible, Sheffield).
Television includes: Hope and Glory, The Rag Nymph, Scully, Coronation Street, The Refuge, Final Run, Albion Market, Children of the North, Nice Town, The Riff Raff Element, Eastenders, Blood on the Dole (part of the Alan Bleasdale season of films for Channel 4), Elidor, Missing Persons, Famous Five.
Film includes: Scrubbers, Priest.

PRODUCERS

The English Stage Company at the Royal Court Theatre

The English Stage Company was formed to bring serious writing back to the stage. The first Artistic Director, George Devine, wanted to create a vital and popular theatre. He encouraged new writing that explored subjects drawn from contemporary life as well as pursuing European plays and forgotten classics. When John Osborne's Look Back in Anger was first produced in 1956 it forced British Theatre into the modern age. Early Court Writers included Arnold Wesker, John Arden, Ann Jellicoe, Edward Bond and David Storey. They were followed by David Hare, Howard Brenton, Caryl Churchill, Timberlake Wetenbaker, Robert Holman and Jim Cartwright.

Many established playwrights had their early plays produced in the Theatre Upstairs including Anne Devlin, Andrea Dunbar, Sarah Daniels, Jim Cartwright, Clare McIntyre, Winsome Pinnock, Martin Crimp and Phyllis Nagy. Theatre Upstairs productions regularly transfer to the Theatre Downstairs, as with Ariel Dorfman's Death and the Maiden, Sebastian Barry's The Steward of Christendem (a co-production with Out of Joint); Martin McDonagh's The Beauty Queen of Leenane (a co-production with Druid Theatre Company), Ayub Khan-Din's East is East (a co-production with Tamasha Theatre Company). 1992 - 1999 have been record-breaking years at the box office with capacity houses for Death and the Maiden, Six Degrees of Separation, Oleanna, Hysteria, The Cavalcaders, The Kitchen, The Queen and I, The Libertine, Simpatico, Mojo, The Steward of Christendom, The Beauty Queen of Leenane, East is East, The Chairs and The Weir.

After four decades the Royal Court's aims remain consistent with thoses established by George Devine. The Royal Court is still a major focus in the country for the production of new work. Scores of plays first seen at the Royal Court are now part of the national and international dramatic repertoire.

Ambassador Theatre Group

Ambassador Theatre Group Ltd (ATG) has three main areas of activity: the ownership and management of theatre buildings, theatre production (in the West End but also nationally and internationally) and the development of new productions.

ATG currently owns and operates the following arts buildings: The Duke of Yorks and the Ambassadors in London, The New Victoria Theatre and Ambassadors Cinemas in Woking, The Victoria Hall and Regent Theatre in Stoke-on-Trent and The Milton Keynes Theatre. It will take over the historic Theatre Royal Brighton in June, and it is anticipated from May 1999, the management of Richmond Theatre.

ATG and its management company the Turnstyle Group Ltd., has a considerable track record in producing and co-producing for the West End and on national and international tours. Recent productions include: Carmen Jones, The Rocky Horror Show, Smokey Joe's Cafe, A Chorus Line, Slava's Snow Show, Late Middle Classes and the Royal Court's Olivier Award winning play The Weir. Currently in rehearsal is the first revival in 40 years of the fifties musical The Pajama Game and a new musical celebrating soul music, Soul Train.

In 1998 Sonia Friedman joined the Ambassador Theatre Group as Producer where she is responsible for initiating, developing and producing a wide range of work for theatres across the West End, UK and internationally. It is anticipated that Sonia will initiate, produce and co-produce approximately 25 productions across the UK between 1999 and 2001 including many new plays.

From 1989-1993 Sonia was head of Mobile Productions and Theatre for Young People at the RNT where she was responsible for producing over 30 productions and projects. In 1993 Sonia co-founded Out of Joint with Max Stafford-Clark. Co-productions with the Royal Court, RNT and Hampstead include The Queen and I by Sue Townsend, The Libertine by Stephen Jeffreys, The Steward of Christendom by Sebastian Barry, The Break of Day by Timberlake Wertenbaker, The Positive Hour by April de Angelis, Shopping and Fucking by Mark Ravenhill, Our Lady of Sligo by Sebastian Barry and Blue Heart by Caryl Churchill. She has also produced The Man of Mode, Road and Three Sisters at the Royal Court, and Our Country's Good. In 1994 Sonia also produced Maria Friedman by Special Arrangement at the Donmar Warehouse.

Guy Chapman Associates

Guy Chapman was head of marketing for the Royal Court Theatre for seven years. In1994 he formed Guy Chapman Associates and a subsidary, Chapman Duncan Productions Ltd., to produce and tour new work. This company premiered with Phyllis Nagy's Disappeared, touring for seven weeks as well as playing at the Royal Court Theatre Upstairs. This was followed by Andrew Alty's Something About Us at the Lyric Hammersmith Studio in 1995 and Godfrey Hamilton's Road Movie (Lyric Hammersmith and tour, 1996).

Guy Chapman co-produced Brothers of the Brush at the Arts Theatre in 1996 and Martin and John at the Bush Theatre in 1998.

In 1996 Guy Chapman and Paul Spyker launched Bright Ltd and have produced: James Edwin Parker's Two Boys on a Cold Winter's Night, John Logan's Never the Sinner, Dan Rebellato's Showstopper and The Twilight of the Golds by Jonathan Tolins; all at the Arts Theatre; and Stephen Schwartz's musical Pippin at The Bridewell Theatre.

With G & J Productions, Bright Ltd has co-produced Mark Ravenhill's Shopping and Fucking (Gielgud / Queen's / National tour / New York Theatre Workshop). They also co-produced Jackie Clune's Chicks with Flicks (The King's Head / Tour) and Enda Walsh's Disco Pigs (The Arts Theatre).

Recent co-productions: Crave by Sarah Kane (Chelsea Centre, Traverse, Royal Court Theatre, Berlin Festival and Dublin Festival); Jackie Clune's It's Jackie! (Assembly Rooms Edinburgh / The Drill Hall / National Tour); Sea Urchins (Grace Theatre); Love Upon the Throne (Assembly Rooms, Edinburgh, Oxford Playhouse, Bush Theatre, Comedy Theatre); The Snowman (Peacock Theatre).

Current productions include: Frantic Assembly's Sell Out (with Mark Goucher); Chicks with Flicks in the USA and Austria, The Snowman at The Peacock in November 1999 and an adaptation of Oscar Moore's PWA with Fierce Earth.

Mark Goucher

In 1997 Mark was the joint recipient of The Stage / Barclays Award for special achievement in Regional Theatre and over the last eleven years has co-produced ground breaking productions in the West End.

For the last six years Mark has successfully represented the Reduced Shakespeare Company's productions in the UK with The Complete Works of Shakespeare (abridged) and The Complete History of America (abridged) now in their fourth year at the Criterion Theatre. The Reduced Shakespeare Company has also toured extensively with The Bible, The Complete Word of God (abridged) and, in the autumn their new show Millennium the Musical.

West End co-productions and subsequent tours include: Trainspotting, Shopping and Fucking, Fever Pitch, Steven Berkoff in One Man, Anorak of Fire, Ennio Marchetto and Kit and the Widow. Touring co-productions include Think No Evil of Us: My Life with Kenneth Williams, An Audience with George Melly, Poulter and Duff and Graham Norton.

Mark is also involved as a co-producer in the New Ambassadors' inaugural season with productions of Sell Out by Frantic Assembly and Last Dance at Dum Dum by Ayub Khan-Din.

FOR THE ROYAL COURT THEATRE

DIRECTION
Artistic Director	Ian Rickson
Director	Stephen Daldry
Assistant to the	
Artistic Director	Nicky Jones
Associate Directors	Dominic Cooke
	Elyse Dodgson
	James Macdonald*
	Max Stafford-Clark*
Associate Director Casting	Lisa Makin
Casting Assistant	Julia Horan
Literary Manager	Graham Whybrow
Literary Associate	Stephen Jeffreys*
Resident Dramatist	Rebecca Prichard+
International Associate	Mary Peate
International Administrator	Nathalie Bintener

PRODUCTION
Production Manager	Edwyn Wilson
Deputy Production Manager	Paul Handley
Head of Lighting	Johanna Town
Senior Electrician	Marion Mahon
Assistant Electricians	Michelle Green
	Maeve Laverty
Head of Stage	Martin Riley
Senior Carpenters	David Skelly
	Eddie King
	Terry Bennett
Head of Sound	Paul Arditti
Sound Deputy	Rich Walsh
Company Stage Manager	Cath Binks
Production Assistant	Sue Bird
Costume Deputies	Neil Gillies
	Rose Willis

YOUNG PEOPLE'S THEATRE
Associate Director	Ola Animashawun
General Manager	Aoife Mannix
Writers' Tutor	Noel Greig

ENGLISH STAGE COMPANY
President	Greville Poke
Vice President	Joan Plowright CBE
Council	
Chairman	Sir John Mortimer QC, CBE
Vice-Chairman	Anthony Burton
Members	Stuart Burge CBE
	Stephen Evans
	Sonia Melchett
	James Midgley
	Richard Pulford
	Nicholas Wright
	Alan Yentob
Advisory Council	Diana Bliss
	Tina Brown
	Allan Davis
	Elyse Dodgson
	Robert Fox
	Jocelyn Herbert
	Michael Hoffman
	Hanif Kureishi
	Jane Rayne
	Ruth Rogers
	James L. Tanner

MANAGEMENT
Executive Director	Vikki Heywood
Assistant to the	
Executive Director	Diana Pao
General Manager	Diane Borger
Finance Director	Donna Munday
Finance Officer	Rachel Harrison
Re-development	
Finance Officer	Neville Ayres
Finance & Administration	
Assistant	Eric Dupin

RE-DEVELOPMENT
Project Manager	Tony Hudson
Deputy Project Manager	Simon Harper
Assistant to Project Manager	Monica McCormack

MARKETING
Head of Marketing	Stuart Buchanan
Press Officer	Giselle Glasman
Marketing Officer	Emily Smith
Marketing Intern	Jake Binnington
Box Office Manager	Neil Grutchfield
Deputy Box Office Manager	Terry Cooke
Box Office Sales Operators	Glen Bowman
	Clare Christou
	Valli Dakshinamurthi
	Sophie Dart
	Jane Parker
	Carol Pritchard*
	Michele Rickett*
	Gregory Woodward

DEVELOPMENT
Head of Development	Helen Salmon
Assistant to	
Head of Development	Zoë Schoon
Trusts and Foundations	Susan Davenport*
Appeals Officer	Sophie Hussey
Development Volunteers	Olivia Hill
	Nick Williams

FRONT OF HOUSE
Acting Theatre Manager	Jemma Davies
Acting Deputy Theatre Manager	Gini Woodward
Acting Duty House Manager	Joanna Crowley
Relief Duty House Managers	Neil Grutchfield*
	Marion Doherty*
	Greg Woodward*
Bookshop Manager	Del Campbell
Bookshop Supervisor	Sarah Mclaren*
Maintenance	Greg Piggot*
Lunch Bar Caterer	Andrew Forrest*
Stage Door/Reception	Lorraine Benloss*
	Tyrone Lucas*
	Nettie Williams*
	Benjamin Till*
	Tom Hescott*
	Suzie Zara
Cleaners	Ridgeway Cleaning Services Ltd.
Firemen	Myriad Security Services

* part-time
+ Arts Council Resident Dramatist

Royal Court Theatre
St. Martin's Lane, London, WC2E 4BG
Tel: 0171 565 5050 Fax: 0171 565 5001
Box Office: 0171 565 5000
www.royal-court.org.uk

Thanks to all of our bar staff and ushers

FOR NEW AMBASSADORS THEATRE

RE - BUILDING
THE ROYAL COURT

The Royal Court was thrilled in 1995 to be awarded a National Lottery grant through the Arts Council of England, to pay for three quarters of a £26 million project to completely re-build our 100-year old home. The rules of the award required the Royal Court to raise £7 million as partnership funding.

Thanks to the generous support of the donors listed below and a recent major donation from the Jerwood Foundation, we have very nearly reached the target. The building work is near completion at the Sloane Square site and the theatre is due to re-open in Autumn 1999.

With only £100,000 left to raise, each donation makes a significant difference to the realisation of this exciting project. If you would like to help, or for further information, please contact Royal Court Development on 0171 565 5050.

ROYAL COURT DEVELOPMENT BOARD
Elisabeth Murdoch (Chair), Jonathan Cameron (Vice Chair), Timothy Burrill, Anthony Burton, Jonathan Caplin QC, Victoria Elenowitz, Monica Gerard-Sharp, Susan Hayden, Angela Heylin, Feona McEwan, Michael Potter, Sue Stapely, Charlotte Watcyn Lewis

RE-BUILDING SUPPORTERS INCLUDE:
Jerwood Foundation

WRITERS CIRCLE
BSkyB Ltd
Foundation for Sport and the Arts
News International plc
Pathé
The Eva and Hans K Rausing Trust
The Rayne Foundation
Garfield Weston Foundation

DIRECTORS CIRCLE
The Esmée Fairbairn Charitable Trust
The Granada Group plc
John Lewis Partnership plc

ACTORS CIRCLE
City Parochial Foundation
Quercus Charitable Trust
RSA Art for Architecture Award Scheme
The Basil Samuel Charitable Trust
The Trusthouse Charitable Foundation
The Woodward Charitable Trust

For information about the American Friends of the Royal Court Theatre telephone 001 212 946 5724.

PROGRAMME SUPPORTERS

The Royal Court (English Stage Company Ltd) is supported financially by a wide range of private companies and public bodies. The company receives its principal funding from the Arts Council of England. The Royal Borough of Kensington & Chelsea gives an annual grant to the Royal Court Young Writers' Programme and the London Boroughs Grants Committee contributes to the cost of productions in its Theatre Upstairs.

Major sponsors, foundations and individual supporters include the following:

TRUSTS AND FOUNDATIONS
A.S.K. Theater Projects, LA
Jerwood Foundation
The Peggy Ramsay Foundation
Alan & Babette Sainsbury Charitable Fund
The John Studzinski Foundation

SPONSORS
The Austrian Cultural Institute
Barclays Bank plc
Bloomberg News
The Granada Group plc
Guiding Star Ltd (Jerusalem)
Virgin Atlantic
Business Members
American Airlines
AT&T (UK) Ltd
British Interactive Broadcasting Ltd
BSkyB
Channel Four Television
Davis Polk & Wardwell
Deep End Design
Goldman Sachs International
Heidrick & Struggles
Lambie-Nairn
Lazard Brothers & Co. Ltd
Mishcon de Reya Solicitors
OgilvyOne
Redwood Publishing plc
Simons Muirhead & Burton
Sullivan & Cromwell
J Walter Thompson

INDIVIDUAL MEMBERS
Patrons
Advanpress
Associated Newspapers Ltd
Citigate Communications
Greg Dyke
Homevale Ltd
Laporte plc
Lex Service plc
Barbara Minto
New Penny Productions Ltd
A T Poeton & Son Ltd
Greville Poke
Sir George Russell
Richard Wilson

new **A** MBASSADORS theatre

last dance
at dum dum

>>THURS 8 JULY – SAT 28 AUGUST

BOX OFFICE 0171 836 6111

New play by **Ayub Khan-Din**
Director **Stuart Burge**
Designer **Tim Hatley**
Lighting **Mark Henderson**

Cast includes **Paul Bazely,**
Avril Elgar, Madhur Jaffrey,
Madhav Sharma, Sheila Burrell

Presented by
The Royal Court Theatre, Ambassador Theatre Group,
Guy Chapman and Mark Goucher

First published in 1999 by Oberon Books Ltd.
(incorporating Absolute Classics)
521 Caledonian Road, London N7 9RH
Tel: 0171 607 3637 / Fax: 0171 607 3629
e-mail: oberon.books@btinternet.com

A catalogue record for this book is available from the British
Library.

ISBN 1 84002 113 6

Cover photograph: Dewynters Plc, Tel: 0171 3210488

Cover design: Andrzej Klimowski

Typography: Richard Doust

Printed in Great Britain by MPG Books Ltd, Cornwall.

Werner Schwab

HOLY MOTHERS

(Die Präsidentinnen)

translated by

Meredith Oakes

OBERON BOOKS
LONDON

Characters

ERNA

on a state minimum pension, apron,orthopaedic shoes,
a big grotesque fur bonnet

GRETE

pensioner, quite fat, beehive hairstyle (blonde), tastelessly dressed,
lots of cheap jewellery, heavy make-up

MARIEDL

dressed like a pauper, hair pulled back, feet stuck into far-too-big hiking
boots. She seemsa bit simple at first. She is somewhat younger than the
other two, and this should be seen in her rather hectic movements

THE ORIGINAL BREECH-LOADING
SOUL SOOTHERS
(in the third scene)

The play:

The play concerns the fact that the earth is flat, and that the sun
rises and sets because it revolves around the earth; it concerns the
fact that nothing is willing to be function, only distraction.

The set:

A small kitchen/living room centre stage. Left and right, complete
blackness. The kitchen/living room is lined to the ceiling with junk
(photos, souvenirs, religious kitsch, framed calendar pictures, con-
tainers etc) but is clean and tidy. There is a museum-like feel to the
arrangement of the objects. A small non-naturalistic space there-
fore, nonetheless recognizable as a lower-middle-class kitchen/
living room.

The language:

The language the women create is what they are. It is work to
create (elucidate) yourself, so everything is, by its very nature,
resistance. This should be perceptible as effort in the play.

Scene 1

While the audience take their seats, a broadcast is heard of the pope celebrating mass with a multitude. The telecast ends and the curtain rises.

ERNA's grotesque kitchen/living room. ERNA turns off the TV. MARIEDL is looking for something under the table. GRETE is seated at the table.

ERNA: All those people. All those people coming together and being together and being all as one at the feet of the Holy Father.

GRETE: And isn't the picture wonderful. The colours could have come from life itself.

ERNA: It's tremendously moving, the sense of peace arising out of all those people. Peace is life's goal, and life is people's goal.

GRETE: (*Lifts the tablecloth and speaks to someone under the table.*) Leave the button, Mariedl, I'm really not that bothered about the button. Forget about the button, sit with us. (*To ERNA.*) It's really clever of you, Erna, to have got yourself that lovely fur bonnet, and the colour television. At last you've brought some enjoyment into your home. Now's the time you should open up to life, and give life the chance to make you happy.

ERNA: Yes, those words slip out so easily, but in reality, enjoying life is very hard, when you've saved and saved, until it's right down in your bones. Still perhaps just for once in my life, happiness will find a person like me, who's never done anything except clean other people's filth. (*ERNA stands before the mirror.*) I found this fur bonnet a year ago, in the rubbish. It's unthinkable that someone would have simply thrown this bonnet away, it's much too valuable.

Obviously it must have been young people, venting their malice on this bonnet. (*She turns her back to the mirror and sits down.*) But you wouldn't believe how filthy it was. I was three-and-a-half hours slaving over it, before it was fit to be taken to the police. (*GRETE gestures that she wants to feel the fur of the hat. ERNA bends down to make it easier for her.*) And now a year's gone by and no-one's claimed it. And he was such a nice policeman at the lost property office, he said to me: The reason you're poor is that you're an honest woman. Why not put this bonnet under your Christmas tree, give a little present to yourself for once... I try not to indulge myself in general, but I have to admit, I was truly pleased by that.

GRETE: You shouldn't persist with this dreadful saving, you're not as poor as you used to be, Erna. And life goes on, you know, it goes on faster than we can imagine.

ERNA: So now I've allowed myself the television, though the television is a used television, of course. It's my one gift to myself in return for all I've given. In every other respect I've always had to save on everything in my life, including my child, Herrmann. If you really know how to save, your life can be planned. Everything can be saved on. Instead of coffee filters, for instance, you can take a bit of toilet paper, and instead of toilet paper, you can use newspaper, which can be picked up from the stairwell, where the papers are left out for recycling – actually, as far as I'm concerned, I could just as well do without the coffee altogether, because luckily I can't digest coffee. But Herrmann refuses to eat his roll and liver sausage without a black coffee to flush it down, as he says. The way he says it, it's as if his roll and liver sausage were human excrement and his stomach were the toilet.

MARIEDL: (*Under the table.*) I don't think it's right, Erna, the way you keep saving. You save far too much, you take it much too far. God doesn't want good people to suffer.

ERNA: (*Furious, lifts up the tablecloth.*) It's easy for you to talk, Mariedl dear, but you live alone and there's never been anyone in your life, has there. You travel the world just as you like, in your spare time. You've already been to Lourdes twice this year, and to Medjugorje, and twice to Mariazell. You don't have the responsibility of an uncontrollable child.

GRETE: But your Herrmann is a man, a manly man.

MARIEDL appears, sits down, shrugs her shoulders as if not knowing what to do, and begins rhythmically rocking the upper part of her body back and forth.

ERNA: Yes, he's the picture of a man. Women all turn their heads to look at him, shameless as they are these days. But Herrmann cannot accept anything in this life which is good, or which makes any sense. Up there, I say to Herrmann, up there is where the pictures of my grandchildren will go. (*She points to two white rectangular spaces on the wall.*) But he refuses to do me the honour, he's not going to make any grandchildren. I was keeping five little places free up there, waiting for grandchildren. I've only just now put something else up in three of them, so as not to frighten him. And yet it ought to be so easy, in today's world, for him to have intercourse. People today have intercourse all day. And Herrmann admits, he could have intercourse any time, but he purposely never does have intercourse, because intercourse might actually lead to a pregnancy, which ultimately might lead to a grandchild.

GRETE: Oh, stop it, Erna, your Herrmann is so big and strong. Miss Right will find him in the end.

17

ERNA: Yes, that's my one hope, if I have to go on living, my one hope is that God will do something about Herrmann. (*Weepily.*) He does get about a lot, as a sales representative, something might happen, but then he keeps sending me these dreadful postcards, on the front is a beautiful landscape, and on the back he writes that once again he's had the opportunity of having intercourse, and once again he's made a point of not having intercourse. (*Weeps.*)

GRETE: (*Pats ERNA on the back to calm her.*) But Erna, when Miss Right comes along, she'll just snap up your Herrmann and kiss him. And intercourse will follow by itself. (*She sings.*) Strangers in the night, Exchanging glances, Wondering... (*Stops suddenly.*) But who on earth am I to talk? Look at my life, Erna. At least Herrmann thinks of you and always sends you one of these cards about intercourse, but what about me? My daughter migrated to Australia nine years ago, and even before that, she got herself gutted like a chicken, ovaries, the lot, everything you need for grandchildren. In nine years she's sent me one postcard. Safely arrived and I'm absolutely fine. She wrote me that eight and a half years ago. Lydia is all I have now.

ERNA: But Herrmann shouldn't keep sending me those cards, all about how he's giving up intercourse for good, or having a vasectomy.

GRETE: Yes, Hannelore, my daughter, and besides, she'll be an old bag by now, she'll be getting on for forty by now. But she's always had peculiar ways, a bit like your Herrmann really. Also Hannelore frequently used to forget that she wasn't the daughter of scum. She often behaved as if she'd had no upbringing. She'd smash her face through a window, then calmly eat the broken glass, and then she'd laugh her head off, cutting her face and her bosom. And if I said to her: Well Lore, at least you look like sliced pork now, the men will want you now; well then she'd just go quiet, and suck her thumb, and sleep thirty hours at a time.

ERNA: Yes that is human life. You try your whole life long to steer a proper course through life, then your own flesh and blood turn their backs on all of it, life, humanity, all of it.

GRETE: Anyway, I hope Hannelore will find happiness out there in Australia, if that's how it has to be, with or without the ovaries.

ERNA: Herrmann is so introverted. When he sees a human being, he has to drink a brandy and smoke a cigarette straight away. He says if he doesn't, he'll get eye cancer. Herrmann has a horror of all human beings, and that's why he became a sales representative, in order to meet people, so that every day he's got the perfect excuse for coming home drunk.

MARIEDL: Very many saints have come from people like that, in the time of their youth they hid their face from the world.

ERNA: The time of their youth? But Herrmann's nearly forty.

MARIEDL: Yes, but any day we can feel an inner push, and pop goes the button.

ERNA: One little button going pop wouldn't make much difference to Herrmann. It would take a whole button factory exploding. He can't even stand himself. When he's washing his face at the tap I have to hang the hand-towel over the mirror before he'll go in there. He cuts off half his face when he's shaving, because he won't have a mirror, he says a mirror's disgusting. He says he'll be walking down the street, and the shop windows will start reflecting, so that Herrmann sees Herrmann, and then he throws up on the spot, unless he's drunk. And this is what he's telling me day in day out, and every word he says and every drink he takes, he's shortening my life.

MARIEDL: Those very people are often found by Jesus, or by the Virgin Mary full of grace, the Lord be with you. And from one day to the next, grace will suddenly burst from a sick heart. Just as Saul became Paul, Herrmann could become His man.

ERNA: Yes, that's the very best thing I could hope for, that inside Herrmann everything could be changed utterly. But what can be expected from someone who all day every day turns his back on everything that makes life worth living. And if I try to say a few good words to him, he laughs, and has a shot of bitters or a shot of brandy.

GRETE: People don't understand what life is. When life speaks to people, and gives them good advice, people shake their heads and act like immigrants, No understand, no understand, that's all they can say for themselves. My Lydia's not like that, she understands everything. If I see her eat some strange piece of shit, I say to her, Lydi, don't eat shit. And straight away she lifts up her little head and nods at me. She saw a wooden dachshund do that once, she learned it straight off.

MARIEDL: (*Enchanted.*) Is that really true?

GRETE: Yes, it was a little dachshund on wheels, it had a child with it. You pulled on its lead and it wagged its little tail, and its little head went yesyes, up and down, yesyesyesyesyes. (*GRETE nods vigorously, MARIEDL laughs hysterically.*) It was beautifully painted wood, that little dachshund, and exactly the same size as Lydi, and oh she did like him. And ever since then, she'll nod her head just like him, whenever I say: Lydi, don't eat shit. (*MARIEDL again bursts out laughing, and puts her hands over her mouth.*)

ERNA: That's enough, Grete, I'm not going to listen to any more of your language. You're always entertaining common words on your lips. All we ever hear from you is shit, shit, shit. There are other things people can say, you can say stool, or number two, not this shit, shit, shit all the time.

GRETE: You criticise everything, you always find fault with everything, you spend your whole life pulling everyone down. Then you ask why Hermann won't have intercourse.

ERNA: (*Somewhat subdued.*) But life isn't worth living, is it, if whatever it is you're looking at, suddenly there's a stinking stool next to it. So often it will be one of the few really beautiful things in life, and then no sooner do you reach out and touch it, than once again you've a heap of shit in your hand.

MARIEDL: I don't mind lower words and I don't actually mind a stool. Because what is it, after all, if you didn't know what it is? All it is, is something warm and soft, when it's fresh. (*She draws herself up proudly.*) People always say, Oh no, the toilet's blocked, quick, fetch Mariedl, she does it without. Because they all know I don't put rubber gloves on, when I'm putting my hand down the toilet. (*ERNA is nearly sick, and turns away.*) They all come to me from all the best houses, whenever a blockage occurs. I go into all the best houses and I'm always treated with kindness wherever I go. And anyway, it really doesn't make me sick, when I reach down in the toilet bowl, because I'm offering it up to our Lord

Jesus Christ, who died on the cross for us. And the best people in the best houses always say to me, would I like some rubber gloves, because they're beautifully mannered well brought up people. But I always say NO, because if the Lord God created the world, He also created human excrement.

ERNA: My God, Mariedl, you really are a filthy cow, you'll have to forgive me, but don't go on please. It's bad enough people having to defecate, and the wicked feelings they so often have. So many times I've asked myself, why does mankind have to have a bum. It's not a thing of beauty, is it, a bum, yet people worship them and make graven images of them.

GRETE: (*Taking no notice of ERNA.*) And the best people really come to you, do they, and call on you for help?

MARIEDL: Very rich and very fine people have come to me, and once they even fetched me in a great big car to one such afflicted toilet. But they don't exactly have what you'd call a toilet. It's very nice what they have, it doesn't even smell like a toilet, it smells just the same as rich ladies do. I've been fetched to the toilet twice by the Sunday-school teacher, and once by the priest. And the priest solemnly promised he'd spread the word through all the congregation, all about Mariedl and what I can do, so that other people can also call on me to come to them when they have a blockage in their toilet.

ERNA: I don't understand that. My toilet bowl is never blocked. It's because people are so thoughtless, I expect, and put the wrong things down, because it isn't easy to block one of those bowls with a stool on its own. I often do quite a large, hard one, because of worrying about Herrmann which presses it all together inside me. What you have to do is give it a firm shove with the toilet brush and flush twice.

But of course you mustn't put too much toilet paper down, because then, anything can happen. Herrmann always gets cross with me, when he's just passed a stool, and I'm listening at the door for how many pieces of paper he's tearing off. But I say to him, it's important; first, because it's a chance to save, and second because it's dangerous if the paper gets all mixed up with one of his bad, sticky jobs. But he just laughs, and has another drink.

GRETE: (*Interested, to MARIEDL.*) What things do rich people put down their toilets that obstruct them so dreadfully?

MARIEDL: There was a jam jar once, with red worms in it for the aquarium fish, and a whole chicken another time, but I think it must have been smelly ever before they put it down the toilet. Books there have been, with pictures of naked people, and underwear, bloodstained or soiled. (*ERNA is practically being sick.*) Don't look so tragic, Erna, you take everything in life so seriously. Life is honest, that's all, and shows people what we consist of. Once you've reached down a toilet bowl, soon all your dreadful fears have gone, and then it's just the same as shaking someone's hand. (*ERNA is nearly sick.*)

GRETE: When it's Lydia's jobs it never bothers me either, because I always know exactly what she's eaten. But people today eat all kinds of things, with all the rich food available. Even the lowest types can purchase anything they fancy.

ERNA: I couldn't do it. I simply couldn't. It would simply make me throw up. I'd heave my guts out. I retch when I so much as brush my teeth. And then when Herrmann sees me brushing my teeth and retching, he pretends to retch as well. He deliberately imitates those inevitable human sounds of someone retching. And he deliberately fools about for so long, pretending he's retching, that finally up comes all his roll and liver sausage. And then do you know what he says to me, the sod, he says to me, You see mum, I told you I don't like liver sausage.

GRETE: Nonsense Erna, why do you have to live in this state of perpetual exaggeration? Herrmann's a big fine man, a marvellous figure of a man, and that's the truth. All he needs is the right woman. If I were a young girl today – well, who knows what might happen, love goes on oiled wheels today. (*Giggles.*)

ERNA: I don't know, Grete, I really don't, conversing with you, it always comes back to sex or heaps of shit. I simply cannot reconcile my belief in God with sex and a little heap of shit. Don't think badly of me if I say this, but our Grete's always been a naughty girl, haven't you. After all, you've been married twice, and your front door hasn't always shut properly either, when it should have.

GRETE: Why should I have to take whatever your dirty mind dumps on the table in front of me, Erna. I was only having these thoughts about Herrmann because when I'm at my window, watching to see the pigeons don't eat the birds' food, I often catch sight of him down in the street...

MARIEDL: What have you got against pigeons? Pigeons are heaven's creatures too.

GRETE: Oh come on Mariedl, really... (*Makes a cuckoo sign at MARIEDL, twirling her finger at her temple.*) Anyway, when I see Herrmann, all big and blond and blue-eyed, I often think what a nice ambience Herrmann's got. Hermann sets me off remembering the sins of my youth. (*Smiles roguishly.*)

MARIEDL: But why have pigeons got no rights in your birdbox? Pigeons are birds.

GRETE: Oh what's the matter with your brains, Mariedl? What on earth do you know about nature? Pigeons completely destroy a window birdbox. Pigeons eat young tits. Lydi gets worn out by those vermin. You should see what it's like, the pounding of her little heart, when the pigeons have upset her, then you wouldn't talk such rubbish.

ERNA: I believe in every living thing being treated well in this world. I'm the first one to feel the horror, when they show on television all the dreadful things that happen. But it was very good what the Bundespresident said in his latest speech. He said he ranged himself on the side of peace and forgiveness. I always say forgiveness is the most important thing on this earth. I'm always able to forgive Herrmann, for everything. When he's yet again abused his body with alcohol, I always say to him, Herrmann, a mother always forgives. But when I forgive him, he always picks up the bottle and drinks, he doesn't even bother with a glass.

MARIEDL: We must always keep our engine of brotherly love running. Whenever I'm able to help someone, happiness steps in through the door of my heart. And if there's ever a time when nobody's needing Mariedl's busy hands, I sit sadly in my room. I'm not very fond of being in my room, that's why I only need a small room, because I'm not at home in a room. So it's lucky that busy hands with brotherly love in them are needed all over the world. My children are all the people I've been privileged to help. Yes, those are my children, and they're all my friends. When they see Mariedl, they say: Ah, Mariedl, are you off again so soon? She works so hard, everyone likes a person like that, and she does it without. (*Jumps up suddenly and shouts.*)

Everyone has a place in their heart for Mariedl,
because of her many good deeds –

ERNA: Yes, yes, we know what a hard-working soul you
are. And you'll get your reward one day. Faith is the
only bridge across this valley of tears. But you're
making the same mistake as me now, you're taking
life too seriously. Not like our Grete, she's been
clever with her life, Grete's had her fun.

GRETE: (*Furious.*) Don't you think you're being rather
nasty? How can you be so nasty behind that laughing
face of yours? Do you think my life has all been one
big barrel of laughs? First I was divorced, then I was
widowed. Do you think marriage is one great big
pleasure trip? What about Kurti, my first husband?
And Hannelore? What do you imagine it's like when
you know, because you can't help knowing, that
your very own husband is punishing your very own
daughter in your very own bed? What about that, for
God's sake?

What you do is, you wait and see, you wait and see
what providence has in mind for people. But you
have to give providence the space to work, until you
finally find out what it's going to be. And at last,
when providence is finished, life becomes much less
painful. Because what's the use of getting so worked
up, you can't change providence, can you. You can't
just grab hold of providence by the throat and say to
it, make me happy. (*She throttles an imaginary throat.*)

No, and in a way I understand about Kurti and
Hannelore. Beautiful memories are so much a part of
love. Kurti often said to me, Hannelore's as beautiful
now as you were, when you were a girl. Of course it
was wrong, what went on there, and anyway
Hannelore was too young at that stage. But you have
to understand Kurti as well. He was such a handsome

officer in the war, he was so proud, and he must have
felt, when we had those victories at the beginning,
that the whole world was going to belong to someone
like him. The whole of the rest of his life he never
got rid of that taste he had for victory. And then when
Hannelore went off to Australia, he divorced me and
married that Chinese or Thailander, whatever she is.
I've never understood that, what he could have seen
in a slit-eyed eighteen-year-old.

ERNA: The physical is mankind's tragedy. Even good
people are often completely destroyed by lust. When
you're young, and the world breaks in on your
humanity with its physicality, as often as not it's the
physicality that drives the humanity out of the world.

GRETE: Yes, and because life brings all these
experiences along with it, I've totally turned my
back on love now, though I still have opportunities.
These days, and with a light heart, Grete just says
NO... And if those old warm feelings still
occasionally come up, I go out and buy myself a hot
dog and a piece of emmenthal, and a gherkin and
a small bottle of beer, and life soon smiles again.

ERNA: You can make wonderful savings on food. I'll
tell you who's cheap – Wottila. He has liver sausage
on permanent special offer. There's nowhere you can
buy liver sausage as cheap as at Karl Wottila. I can't
even remember how long it is I've been buying liver
sausage from Wottila. Wottila actually told me once,
liver sausage has given him a great deal to be
thankful for, businesswise, and because of that, all
his life he's kept the liver sausage down, pricewise.
It's been a kind of a vow with him, he made that
quite clear to me. He promised himself that if ever
in life he achieved his own butcher's shop, he'd keep
the price of liver sausage right down in the basement

for a lifetime. Yes, and it came to pass he did achieve his own butcher's shop, and now the people stand in line to obtain their liver sausage cheap. He's also had a very interesting life, Wottila, he was actually born in Poland, he told me all about it, when he was visiting here.

GRETE: Did Wottila come and visit you?

ERNA: Very much so, and he brought me some flowers and a kilo of mince.

MARIEDL: Wottila is a very religious man. Wottila has a very strong faith.

GRETE: Erna, Erna, he's the one for you, even if he is a Pole. But a non-smoker, Erna, and he's teetotal. Might he not be visiting you again?

ERNA: (*Weepily.*) We were sitting right here, in this very spot, talking together, it was beautiful, everything we said was so full of meaning. Then Herrmann, the sod, came into the room. He'd just finished sleeping it off, and he says, aha, aha, and he's making his nostrils go funny, aha, he says, what's that stink of liver sausage, quick, I need a drink – I was so ashamed, I was sitting there wishing the ground would swallow me up. But Wottila kept very calm. All he said was, he didn't think from the look of him that Herrmann was ever likely to gain eternal salvation. He said you could see it straight away from Herrmann's face. He said there wasn't enough matter in it, and no eternal flame would light up in his head.

GRETE: Go on Erna, you don't have to believe everything Wottila says.

ERNA: Wottila's had years of experience. That's his hobby, he studies the faces of all his meat customers. He told me once I'm a good woman but I've got an unhappy life, and that was exactly right.

MARIEDL: We should never ever give up on someone. We should always stay with them, and try to shepherd them with foresight and hindsight in the direction of faith, that's what the priest said.

ERNA: Wottila's a strict man, because he lives alone. Anyway I said to him, I can't just push my own son out the door. But also you have to remember that Wottila had a vision once, in the middle of a dark wood, when he came to a clearing. He was just about to light up a cigarette and take a shot of bitters when suddenly the Virgin Mary appeared to him. He got such a shock he fell over backwards. She was ten-and-a-half feet tall and beautifully dressed, and she said to him, smoking and drinking are sins against health, give them up, go back and do penance, and tell this to all the world. After that, Wottila fell into a coma which lasted several hours. And when he came to, he found a bunch of white roses beside him, and a bottle of mineral water. So he created a shrine in that place, and ever since then he's only ever drunk mineral water, perhaps at most a milk coffee in the mornings, but never bitters, never again.

GRETE: That may well be true, but Wottila isn't right about everything. You told me yourself how Wottila once said that Herrmann should eat plenty of liver sausage, on account of his sick alcoholic liver. And that, my dear Erna, is wrong, totally wrong, it's been scientifically proved. I asked a real gynaecologist, my gynaecologist.

ERNA: Scientifically – scientifically, well, scientists are unable to agree among themselves, though most believe in God, even Albert Einstein. That's what the priest said. Besides, I don't credit everything the scientists say, it simply doesn't work like that. And

don't try and tell me Wottila's liver sausage isn't good
for Herrmann's liver, because I refuse to believe it.
If you'd seen how Wottila works with sausages, he's
so upright and so clean, you can be absolutely sure
no uncleanliness would ever get in, and none of those
poisonous additives that might harm people. Yes, and
your gynaecologists can all go and jump in the lake,
they can't even think straight, because all they're
doing, day in and day out, is dealing in sex.

GRETE: Oh really, Erna... Really... (*Laughs.*) You won't
hear a word against Karl Wottila, will you, because
you're in love with him, because he's one of the
God squad.

MARIEDL: (*Very loudly.*) We don't say God squad.

ERNA: (*Jumps up.*) Yoouu... you're a Nazi, you're a
divorcée, you're not even allowed to take proper
communion.

GRETE: (*Jumps up.*) You're divorced as well, you old
Bible-basher.

ERNA: Yes, but I was the innocent party. I can eat the
communion.

GRETE: Yees, because your twat's all wrong, nothing
will go in there except a bit of liver sausage.

MARIEDL begins to cry.

ERNA: Sex... sex, that's all you know. You're a whore,
a Nazi Hitler whore.

GRETE: Nazi... Nazi, what do you know about Nazis.
Everyone was Nazis then. And if I'm a whore, you're
a nun with a sewn-up twat.

ERNA: (*Shouts.*) The truth, the truth is, no-one was
a Nazi, a handful at most. Not in this country, nooo,

that was Hitler, he was evil, he misled people. And
that's exactly what our Bundespresident's been
saying. But what's the point my talking to someone
who doesn't even get herself to church half the time.
People who reject the mass are only fit for the meat
grinder, that's what Wottila says.

GRETE: (*Full of hate, steps up to ERNA.*) Yees, and what
a shame it is, that Hitler never caught up with your
Polish liver-sausage bishop back then.

*ERNA shrieks and attacks GRETE. They have a long and
merciless fight. MARIEDL tries to pray out loud but is
repeatedly interrupted by her own sobbing. Suddenly, as if
turned to stone, the combatants stop. Embarrassed, they loosen
their grip on each other and begin to tweak themselves back
into shape. MARIEDL calms down and picks up the pieces of
hair from GRETE's beehive. ERNA and GRETE sit on the
floor completely disorientated. After a while, ERNA gets up
and with MARIEDL's help, lifts fat GRETE to her feet.*

ERNA: What a stupid fuss about nothing.

MARIEDL: (*Zealously tidying the room.*) Now you've
got to be friends again, and learn to love thy
neighbour again.

GRETE: You should learn to accept other people's
opinions, Erna, that's what we have to be able to
do, and the Bundespresident said that as well.

ERNA: Yes, but so should you.

GRETE: What do you mean? Do you think I'm not
a Christian? I am a Christian, you know, but it's
harder for me than it is for ordinary people. And
why? Because of Lydi, of course. Am I supposed to
leave her all alone, while I go off to mass? That's the
problem, don't you see, I've always wanted to say
that to you, Erna. And I couldn't expect a bright

little thing like Lydi to stay sitting still all that time
in the church, even supposing they'd let her in. So
what am I supposed to do with Lydi on a Sunday?

ERNA: I can understand it's a real problem, Grete.
I really didn't mean it like that.

GRETE: And I didn't mean what I said about Wottila.
There's nothing the matter with his liver sausage,
even Lydi eats a little bit of it sometimes, and she's
very fussy.

MARIEDL: Now brotherly love is back in place. Now
you have to kiss each other and it will all be all
right again. (*She pushes ERNA's and GRETE's heads
together. At first GRETE and ERNA are unwilling, then they
fall into each other's arms.*)

ERNA: Let's put all life's filth out of our minds. The
best thing we can do is enjoy ourselves. Herrmann's
in the pub, your daughter's in Australia and
Mariedl's all right, isn't she? Let's forget all about
problems and politics.

GRETE: You're right, why shouldn't a couple of old
Blunzen like us be having some fun as well? I'll go
across and get some wine.

MARIEDL: Just remind me, what is a *Blunze*?

GRETE: A blood sausage.

ERNA: Ha ha, which brings us back to Karl Wottila.

Scene 2

*Again, ERNA's kitchen/living room. The arrangement is still the same
but the space looks somehow different. Its social characteristics have
become blurred and have taken on a more festive character, more like
the atmosphere of a fairground. On the table is a small open wine
bottle with three exceedingly large glasses and a breadbasket with dry*

rolls. The TV is on and shows the test pattern. Everyone is comfortable and sipping the wine.

ERNA: I can say to him a hundred times, come and sit down Herrman and watch the film, it has a meaning, it will be good for your conscience. But he purposely won't watch the film.

MARIEDL: Films are nearly all beautiful. The mountains and the sea, and people kiss each other on the mouth and have real babies. And there are always very difficult difficulties, which are cleansed out of the world by the good people.

ERNA: A good film shows life as it could be, if people would only be kind to one another. It's important to show good people in films, in order to make people kinder, especially the young towards the old.

GRETE: And above all, a film has to have some fun in it, to give life a bit of relaxation.

ERNA: Yes, daily life needs a little relief. But I also like a problem film with a meaning, because of the cross I bear like a punishment in life because of Herrmann –

MARIEDL: Cheerfulness is fertilizer for the soul, if it's tasteful. The priest says, the shepherd loves his sheep when they frolic.

GRETE: (*Raises her glass.*) Cheers! (*Sings.*) Roll out the barrel, We'll have a barrel of fun...

ERNA: (*Laughs.*) You do make me laugh, Grete, you've really got the art of entertainment in your nature. It's another thing we must to be able to do, is have a good time. But you're not as oppressed by your missing child as I am with Herrmann.

GRETE: We're not having any more Herrmann sagas. (*Sings.*) Did you think I'd crumble, Did you think

I'd lay down and die, Oh no not I ...(*MARIEDL applauds rapturously.*)

ERNA: (*Mildly.*) Don't make fun of me, Grete.

GRETE: Yes, but we're celebrating, aren't we, for once, the hat, and the colour television, so that's enough – (*To MARIEDL.*) Come on Mariedl, sing us a happy song.

MARIEDL: (*Thinks. Sings.*) My ding-a-ling, My ding-a-ling, Having such fun with my ding-a-ling...

ERNA: Well I never...

MARIEDL falls silent. ERNA and GRETE look at her astonished. Suddenly GRETE starts laughing and shrieking.

GRETE: She doesn't know what she's singing, hahaha...

ERNA: You shouldn't always think the worst Grete. It's a popular song, that's all.

GRETE: Well, what would you say is meant by a ding-a-ling? You're not as loopy as her.

ERNA: Yes, but you shouldn't be taking it on such a vulgar level. It's intended to be symbolic, that's the level it's meant on.

MARIEDL understanding nothing of this, shakes her head in bewilderment.

GRETE: Rubbish, when I say something, I say it, and when I celebrate something, I celebrate it. My inner self is thinking back to the times when Grete still used to be in love. And my inner self is celebrating, with a glass of wine.

MARIEDL: Mariedl can always tell when the hearts of others are swelling up and bouncing like a

34

rubber ball. (*She stands up and tries out a couple of dance steps, but immediately sits down again.*)

ERNA: The most I allow myself to think is, that one day, Wottila and I might go to Rome. An *urbi et orbi* in St Peter's square, that would be wonderful, or even just a trip into the countryside – or a nice party perhaps.

GRETE: Yes. A nice big beerfest would be just the thing for Grete. With lots of people and musicians, all in magnificent costumes. There'd be one musician who's especially big and strong, a handsome devil, he's so powerful, he plays the tuba. And he's winking at me the whole time, what a cheek. You can see straight away he's the biggest rogue out of all those musicians, because he's the only one that's got his sleeves rolled up. And when there's a lull in the music, this handsome one drinks beer out of a huge great tankard and he raises it to Grete. And Grete takes hold of her wineglass and raises that a little bit as well. And without any of the festive gathering being aware of it, there's now been established a line of communication between the stage, where the musicians are, and the little table where Grete is sitting. And suppose there's now a longer pause in the music, and someone gets up on the stage and starts telling jokes. The handsome one, he's called Freddy, now has plenty of time in which to observe Grete. But Grete only looks at him a little bit, because she isn't one of those women who'll be standing there in their combinations the minute a man shows an interest. Nevertheless, Grete can feel how love has crept in the door and is taking hold of her and Freddy.

MARIEDL: Mariedl's allowed to help out behind the bar at the party. She's ever so busy wiping everything

clean, and sometimes she's allowed to serve someone.
Admiring eyes are watching Mariedl's skilful hands
whisking about with the dishcloth. Suddenly a well-
dressed man bursts into the party in a terrible state,
and tells all the people enjoying themselves that the
toilet is blocked, that all the toilets are blocked, and
that human excrement is already rising to the edge
of the toilet bowls.

ERNA: Everyone's allowed to enjoy themselves for
now, because the soul has to have a break. But
before the party, all the good people have been to
mass, because you should give thanks to God before
embarking on a good time and a bit of fun. Wottila's
forehead is still wet with the holy water, when he
arrives at the party with Erna on his arm. And
everyone's holding alcoholic drinks under Wottila's
nose, and unhealthy cigarettes. But all he says, he
says, Think, turn back, and tell this to all the world.
And Erna looks up at him, happily.

*All three women fantasize intermittently with their eyes closed
and their heads laid back.*

GRETE: Meanwhile Freddy's been playing the tuba so
hard, he's carved out some free time. He signals to
the other musicians, they're all attractive, to change
round their music to something without any tuba in
it, because he might not have much time to play the
tuba now. (*Giggles.*)

MARIEDL: Everyone's been drinking lots of good beer,
and eating lots of good meat, and soon they all feel
an urge, a terrific urge, because food desires to depart
from the human body, once the nourishment has been
drawn from it. But what can they do, everything is
blocked, there isn't a single toilet they can use. Also
the tension is mounting, because one toilet has
already overflowed. People are all brandishing their

arms and shouting, Where's Mariedl, she does it without; fetch Mariedl, because the toilet has yet to be blocked that could withstand her.

ERNA: And Erna playfully drinks a glass of wine, and Wottila eyes her in quite a roguish way.

GRETE: Freddy is smiling in definitely a roguish way, but he's very embarrassed. Because he's just got up his courage to come and sit next to Grete. Grete looks at him out of the corner of her eyes and she sees poor Freddy has gone red right up to the roots of his blond hair. Lydi barks out loud under Grete's table, because she's extremely jealous. (*Laughs.*) But Freddy puts his head down under the table and strokes Lydi so delicately, she falls for him as well.

MARIEDL: Mariedl has been discovered among the crowd. Everyone drinks a toast to Mariedl. Hurrah, hurrah, hurrah comes the cheer and they carry her on their shoulders to the toilet. The priest is already there and he's got a roguish smile as well. He's got a new pair of pink rubber gloves in his hand and he's waving them in Mariedl's face. But Mariedl just shakes her head. Then everybody laughs, because they already knew Mariedl would shake her head. And the whole crowd steps aside so Mariedl can get to work. She's already taking off her green waistcoat and rolling up the sleeves of her pink blouse above the elbows.

ERNA: Yes, but meanwhile Erna is eating a smoked meat roll with gherkins which Wottila has bought for her. When Wottila went over to the bar, he sniffed the smoked meat rolls and he said the smoked meat wasn't really proper, not like in his shop. But he said it was better than nothing, and a person shouldn't be fussy. Anyway it tastes good enough to Erna because she's having such a wonderful time, and Wottila looks down, quite human, and he even says perhaps they might have a dance when there's a slow tune.

GRETE: And that Freddy, oh he really can dance. He takes tight hold of Grete and whirls her about underneath the decorations. He knows just what to do, being a musician, but the other girls, with their spotty boys, keep on watching him. And the things he keeps saying in Grete's ear, now it's her turn to blush. And he's already felt her once down there. But poor Lydi. Just for the moment Grete's had to tie her up – outside the room because of the noise. And she's so brave... no barkies, just a little whimper.

MARIEDL: Mariedl is in the midst of her work, but she hasn't found anything yet. There's something deep down which is causing the blockage, and also people have done such a lot of firm hard stools in there, they keep coming to the surface one after another. But then Mariedl feels a thing which is even harder. It's hard and smooth and sort of round. So she manages to get her fingers round it and it's a tin, and what's more, a tin which hasn't been opened. And all the people are applauding as Mariedl holds up the tin in her hands and the water rushes down the toilet. Then the priest says that now the tin belongs to Mariedl, and he throws her a tin opener. He says to her to look for the good which may be inside. Quick as a flash, she's wiped the poo off the tin and it's neatly opened. And there in the open tin is a goulash, and oh it does smell good. And the priest says, it's a Hungarian goulash, a spicy one, and with that, he throws Mariedl a fork and a bread roll.

GRETE: Yes, it's poor Lydi just for now, but little does she know how unbelievably happy she soon will be. Freddy's been feeling Grete more and more, and in addition, he himself is getting quite big inside his trousers. He's been telling Grete all about how he owns a big farm, with lots of people working for him and it's even got its own slaughterhouse. There'll be lots of room for Lydi to be let out, and all the best meat. And he says how Grete would be just the kind of a live wire to be the boss's wife. And Grete can see very clearly that providence is in the process of bringing about exactly the right thing for her. Freddy says to Grete, why don't they go outside and find a quiet spot somewhere. But Grete wags her finger at him and gets a little bit cross. And she says to him, she's serious about him, it's not that she doesn't understand what he's saying, but there's a proper way of doing things. And Freddy-baby respects her for that. You're a woman for life, he says, and he's right. I actually say to him, When you're right, you're right. And he gets even bigger inside his trousers.

MARIEDL: Mariedl dips half her bread roll in her tin of goulash and...

ERNA: Hang on, not yet. (*She glares at MARIEDL.*) It's a slow tune, can't you hear it? (*She lifts her head dreamily.*) At last they're playing something slow... Wottila takes Erna's elbow, and asks if he can have the honour. He tells her straight away, he's not much of a dancer, what with being a God-fearing person and having worked himself up to his own butcher's shop, he's never really had the time to shake a leg. And he even laughs a little bit, and says that if you want to make something of your life, you have to watch every step and watch every mouthful, he says. And Erna knows just what he means, she knows what life is like when you have to save, and her heart grows very soft. And as they're playing the final chords, Wottila says very quietly in Erna's ear, that he has to go into the toilets, because his braces have come undone at the back and he has to fix them, and he might avail himself of the facilities to pass a stool while he's there. Yes, says Wottila, it's a hard life, a bachelor's life. Which goes to show how much trust he's already come to place in Erna, the fact that he can tell her an intimate thing like that.

MARIEDL: Yes, and Mr Karl Wottila is welcome to come, because Mariedl has already unblocked one toilet. And now she's got her strength back, thanks to the goulash. That's the first time it's ever happened to Mariedl that a toilet has turned out to be blocked with something good to eat. There are people standing in a circle all around her, a couple of metres back, which is understandable, because they're put off by the smell. But they don't begrudge her the delicious goulash, you can see that, because of the way everyone is smiling. And now she's finished the goulash, they're all calling out go, go, go, and cheering her on to the next toilet. And the priest's already standing there laughing ever so roguishly, and waving the rubber gloves. And all the happy people are calling out all at once, Mariedl does it without, Mariedl does it without... And already Mariedl is thrusting her hand deep into the toilet, she knows what to do, Mariedl does. In no time at all, she's fished out the sodden toilet paper and all the soft stool, and once again, she feels something hard... It feels like glass, she says to herself, and whoosh, up it comes, and once again the water's rushing down the toilet, it's a joy to hear it, and what has Mariedl got in her hand? It's a bottle of beer, a full bottle of beer, and once again, it hasn't been opened. The perfect thing with goulash, thank you Father, she says, because now she understands exactly what's going on, the priest wanted to give her a surprise, and he's done just like the Easter bunny and hidden a little present in the toilet, a lovely bottle of Styrian beer. And now Mariedl knows why the third toilet is blocked. Because probably that naughty priest has put something down that one as well. I'm really curious to know what's hidden in the third toilet.

ERNA: Yes, but now it's time to give Mariedl's toilet a rest, at last, because an honest man like Wottila deserves to have his say as well.

GRETE: What about Freddy? What's he supposed to do with his hard-on, pickle it? Wottila is sitting on the toilet which Mariedl's made available. So it's Freddy now, and Grete.

GRETE closes her eyes and smiles dreamily. ERNA shakes her fist at GRETE and glares at her for a long time, full of hatred. MARIEDL happily drinks an imaginary bottle of beer.

Now where was I, the finger. Grete wags her finger at Freddy, just as if he were a little boy, and what does he do, the rogue? He shows a finger to her as well, but it's his finger. And Freddy has a big round forefinger, and what does that rogue do with it? No sooner has he waltzed Grete out of the spotlight than he puts that finger up Grete's privates. And it gives her such a thrill, but she has to bring her darling back to earth again. And Freddy understands her straight away, of course he does, he doesn't want a whore for a wife. So Grete whips out Freddy's finger, and Freddy looks at his finger with an expression of happiness on his face, and presses his lips to it. Yes, yes, Grete says to her darling, now you've had your finger in Grete's treasure chest, and it's nothing like the dead chickens you find in some women's underwear, is it. And what does Freddy-baby do? There on the spot, he asks Grete to marry him. But Grete knows her way around, so

all she says is, she'd like to dance for a bit, and
perhaps later on there'll be an answer that Grete
can give to Freddy.

MARIEDL: And the beer is like the elixir of life to
Mariedl –

ERNA: Wait a minute, you're not getting away with
that. Just shut up, Mariedl. Because how could
anyone possibly think Wottila would still be on the
toilet, there's nothing the matter with his intestines
you know. As soon as he gets back he says to me,
he did a quick firm stool, because he's not a sick
pig like those people that smear filthy words about
everything on toilet walls. If anything, he says,
the disgusting things written there in that toilet
actually made his bowels move all the faster. The
pope, the Bundespresident, everything's dragged
through the mud in there, says Wottila, and he even
gives Erna a kiss on the nose. But a lot depends on
having the proper nourishment of course, he says,
bad stools are the result of negligent eating. And
people who have bad stools wind up spending a lot
of time on the toilet, and then along come the bad
thoughts that those kind of people have, who write
up all their disgusting filth on toilet walls. Wottila
is a very clever man. For instance, he says it would
be a good idea to put up a simple cross on the
wall facing the toilet, or a photograph of the
Bundespresident, because in schools and public
buildings they have photographs like that. It would
remind people of their own unworthiness, it would
make people remember that they themselves are
nothing but little heaps of shit, and that they
shouldn't write on the walls. But what can you say
about a world, he says, where bad substances have
no sooner collected in the human body than they
start trying to immortalise their sickness all over

their surroundings. Wottila's so right in everything he says, he definitely has a calling, in fact he's now become a member of the church council. I'm now responsible for worldly issues and for the entire development of the church, he says.

MARIEDL has been listening raptly. During ERNA's explanation she has moved her chair very close to ERNA's. Now she pulls it away with a lot of noise and commotion.

MARIEDL: I'm really glad Mariedl solved all the toilets' problems, because Mr Karl Wottila is a man who really inspires respect in people, especially now he's on the church council... (*Reflectively at first, then suddenly bursting out.*) But not even Mr Church Councillor Wottila knows what kind of a surprise is hidden in the third toilet. Only God knows that, and the priest, and perhaps the angels, oh and of course the Virgin Mary. So there's a huge crowd already waiting at the third toilet, and they shout their loudest when strong Mariedl puts her whole arm down the toilet, right to the armpit hairs. But there was nothing hard or smooth down in the hole. That's funny, thinks Mariedl, perhaps it really is just stools blocking the toilet, but then I saw the priest was laughing really roguishly again and he said I should reach further down. You are a rascal, Mariedl says to the priest, and she reaches down again through everything which is in the toilet bowl. And then she feels such a strange thing and she pulls it out, and it's a little package wrapped in a little plastic bag so the pretty wrapping paper won't get wet in the toilet. And now everyone's clapping and singing, For she's a jolly good fellow, for she's a jolly good fellow, for she's a jolly good fellow, and so say all of us. And the people are overjoyed at seeing Mariedl so happy. And the priest says the little package is in recognition of all

Mariedl's hard work. Quickly she opens it. And what's inside? It's French perfume, real, so Mariedl can smell nice.

GRETE: A woman like Grete doesn't need perfume, although she gets it all the time as presents from her admirers. But Grete's own body smell is so good already that she practically never uses foreign scents. And Freddy has just said I smell as good as his favourite meal, roast pork and roast potatoes. And that's an important quality in a wife, that she smells at least as good as her husband's favourite meal. But now Grete has a tough decision to make and a huge responsibility: should she give her hand to Freddy for all the rest of her life? She goes a little distance away from the party, so she can talk about it to Lydi, but Lydi's caught up in a terrible conflict of her own. On the one hand, there's all that space to run around in, and the lovely meat, but on the other hand, she's going to have to share her mistress with Freddy. It isn't easy for Lydi, you have to understand that, even though Lydi is so taken with Freddy as well. And while Grete is standing there, with absolutely no idea any more of what decision she should latch on to, all of a sudden Lydi starts nodding her little head saying yesyesyesyesyes. Now Grete knows she can grab hold of Freddy, with God's blessing. And all at once she feels a great surge of happiness in her heart and she walks back into the party with a firm step. Freddy's already coming towards her, and his eyes are electric with suspense and fear, and yearning and desire. He goes down on his knees to her, and he says that if she hits him with a no, he'll kill himself. Oh darling, you great big silly, says Grete running her fingers through his golden hair, I think it's a yes, says Grete. He jumps up as if a wild boar had just bitten him, and would you believe it, he's yelling at the top of his

voice, she'll have me, she'll have me, and next minute
he's up on the stage. All his musician friends are
shaking him by the hand, congratulating him on the
lovely Grete, and he grabs his tuba and plays on it
till it practically explodes. Everyone at the party is
happy, and they dance around the handsome young
couple. But many of the men are quite dashed,
because they wanted Grete for themselves, but Grete's
made her choice and she's going to have to send
those disappointed men on their way, because she's
chosen her one and only, and he's beyond compare.
(*GRETE is exhausted and happy. She wipes the sweat off her face.*)
Aaah, that was good...

MARIEDL: Mariedl opens the bottle of perfume and
takes a quick sip...

ERNA: I never knew you had such a rude sewage outlet
of a mouth, Mariedl. Can't you see that Erna and
Wottila have been sitting closer and closer together?
You ought to realise there's something so wonderful
happening that it has to be told. (*She lifts her head and
becomes dreamy again.*) The two of them are eating
another smoked meat roll as well, except that now
Erna's having a milk coffee with hers, because
another glass of wine might send her feelings
stampeding over the edge of the abyss. And besides,
Wottila has taken one of Erna's work-roughened hands
and is holding it between the two of his, and he's
looking with respect at her worn fingers. He says the
Mother of God who appeared to him in the clearing
strongly resembled Erna, just as she also resembled
his mother, except the Mother of God was much more
magnificent clotheswise, and had these crazy lighting
effects around her. When Erna hears this, she
immediately feels as if her inner self is shooting
straight up to heaven. I'm honoured, she says, it's
all she's capable of saying, she's so overwhelmed.

And Wottila says: There has to be a deeper symbolic
significance, doesn't there, if my mother and the
Mother of God and my best customer, Frau Erna, all
look practically the same. I'm going to have to do
something about this, thus speaks my soul, he says.
Yes, says Erna, but what can we do? Well, possibly,
marriage might be a good idea, says Wottila, and also
from a business point of view, because a butcher's
shop needs a woman's touch, he says. Yes, I can
understand that, says Erna. Then Wottila takes a deep
breath and says: His Will be done, I'm putting my
meat business in your hands, Frau Erna Wottila. Frau
Erna Wottila, whispers Erna, completely overcome.
And Wottila solemnly announces: I think we might
risk another smoked meat roll and a glass of wine.
Yes, says Erna, and with a boiled egg on it this time,
please. That's two shillings extra, he says, but this day
is so special, it's right in its way. And with real
distinction in his stride, he goes over to the bar and
orders his order.

*MARIEDL puts up her hand like a child in school, while
sticking her other finger up her nostril. She is disregarded.*

GRETE: Grete has a great bundle of happiness right now
as well. Freddy is totally wild about Grete, he has to
keep adjusting his lederhosen, they're squeezing
him so tight. But he keeps control of himself like
a good boy, because he honours and respects her
womanhood. And Grete's always been one who looks
to the future, the main thing she's thinking about now
is the cut of her wedding dress and what she'll give
Lydi for a wedding present. A veal chop, that goes
without saying, but there ought to be something
special as well. Maybe a new doggie bed.

ERNA: In Erna and Wottila a deep peace has broken
out. The two of them can't think of anything else

that needs to be said. Erna's feeling a bit sick because of all the smoked meat rolls, but when you've had too many good things to eat for once, it's a pleasant form of sickness. Naturally, Erna is thinking of the future to come, because there's a big responsibility lying in wait for her. After all, she's changing from a cleaner into a businesswoman, it's a big transition. And she's going to have to be even more careful in everything she does, because her whole life will have gained in importance. When someone's in the business world they can't simply go about with anyone and everyone just as they please, because when the wave of responsibility hits the deck of the ship of life, then there's all sorts of things you can no longer allow yourself. A businesswoman must keep dirt and filth at arm's length from her life.

MARIEDL is growing more restless, she's putting her hand up again and scraping at the floor with her mountain boots.

GRETE: Yes, and Grete knows as well that her fastidiousness is going to have to come out even more strongly than before. As mistress of a proper estate you become even more of a target for life's filth. And Lydi has new responsibilities also, she's going to have to become a real watchdog, there'll be no more eating shit, because she's going to have to guard Grete and Freddy from all the unpleasantness of the world. Bad elements come piling in on you, when you move up and make something better of yourself. We're going to need a lot of security arrangements in our new life.

ERNA: The man in the street envies you everything you've got, when you've worked yourself up to something and own your own business. Because you're bound to have a bit of nice jewellery, and

maybe even a shiny car. Which means that a person
who's worked hard can make frequent visits to
Lourdes and Medjugorje, only not in a stinking bus.
But it's always the same. You finally get your reward
for a life spent hard at work, and people straight away
start throwing filth at you. And those elements are
going to keep on doing it until everything true, and
everything fine, is drowned in urine and excrement.

MARIEDL: (*Wriggling.*) Meee, it's my turn to...

GRETE: Oh go on. Get your filthy imaginings out of
your system. Then Erna and I can start thinking
about serious problems.

MARIEDL: (*Agitated, scratching herself all over.*) The people
have all left the toilet again. Everyone's gone. No-one
remains behind except Mariedl. Mariedl stands there
with her empty perfume bottle, because she's drunk it
all, and inside she smells like all the rich ladies in the
world all put together. But on the outside, she's still
covered in poo, and it makes her a little bit sad. My
beauty lies in my soul, she thinks to herself, but the
trouble is, my soul is such a long way in. The soul is
feeding on eternity, but meanwhile the only thing
anyone sees is your body all your life. And she's cut
herself on the tin of goulash. And the beer's all gone,
she's drunk all that as well, and Mariedl feels really
sick. Because Hungarian goulash and French perfume
don't really mix well in the body. It can be very
lonely in a toilet when you're all alone and you
haven't got anything big or small you need to do. So
poor Mariedl pulls herself together and washes off the
worst of the stool. She wants to be with all the other
people pursuing their happiness at the party. So she
goes in there and warms herself to the merry sound
of the music. She sees Grete, hopping about and
giggling because that big blond fatso is trying to put

his finger up her dress again. She sees Erna and Wottila pledging their love with a cup of milk coffee. And everyone's got so much joy in their heart it's almost running over, like a blocked toilet. But life obeys its own laws, and conjures up mortal danger from its calm surface. Outside the party, a taxi has pulled up, and out of it get two people, a man and a woman. They haven't even paid the driver, and he's running after them, shouting: Oi, where's my fare? But the man just says, the old women inside will cough up for it, so the three of them go in. And they see a little dog tied up, a dachshund, it's called Lydi, and the woman gives it such a terrible kick that it falls down and doesn't get up again.

GRETE: Aaaaaah, that bitch, that whore, who is she?

ERNA is listening with interest and signals to GRETE to be quiet. GRETE carries on sobbing quietly.

ERNA: Go on, Mariedl.

MARIEDL: (*Leans back and closes her eyes.*) Grete recognises Hannelore straight away, even at a distance. (*GRETE sobs harder.*) Grete turns as white as a sheet and all she can do is stammer: Where is Australia, anyway? Hannelore comes straight up to Grete and without saying a word, she gives her a couple of mighty whacks across the face, and Grete's false teeth fall out and her wig's been knocked sideways. Then she says to Grete that this irritating man behind her is a taxi driver wanting to be paid and that Grete will have to pay him, because from now on, all bills are going to have to be paid out of Grete's meagre life savings. Grete can only howl, and the dribble runs down from her mouth.

GRETE yells and hurls herself at MARIEDL. ERNA is too fast for GRETE and holds her back.

ERNA: Don't try to prevent Mariedl from looking into reality, she might be going to see my life's happiness with Wottila. We have to be able to endure the truth, Grete, we have to stand on our feet staring the truth in the face, even if our feet are swollen... Go on, Mariedl.

GRETE has collapsed into her chair and is shaking. MARIEDL closes her eyes again and speaks.

MARIEDL: Freddy's quite lost his appetite for sticking his finger in Grete's bum. He's looking with embarrassment at the false teeth lying on the dirty floor. And because he finds it all so distressing, he takes his money out. The taxi driver keeps laughing stupidly all the time and he asks Freddy what sort of a necrophiliac Freddy is, and Grete's sitting there all dishevelled. Freddy puts down two banknotes on the table and says he's really been stitched up by the old bag. Then Hannelore laughs out loud and whacks Grete again a couple of times and her wig falls right off. The same people who previously were gathered around the surprise toilets are now standing around Grete as if she were a toilet that's blocked. And one of them says, look, that woman has shat herself. Freddy gets still more uncomfortable. He puts another two notes down on the table, then he stands up, finishes his beer and goes over and joins the onlookers. Then someone comes in, and throws something down on the floor, and says: Whose dead dog is this?

GRETE: Lydiii. (*GRETE is having convulsions. She is clenching her fists and her face is distorted.*)

ERNA: Life brings up many a flower from hell into this vale of tears.

MARIEDL: Meanwhile people are getting restless again, because there isn't anything more for them to look at. Grete has buried herself under an old newspaper and doesn't move. Hannelore is on the telephone to the lunatic asylum. But on the far side of the room, a crowd quickly gathers because Herrmann is stumbling among the tables. He's big and bloated and completely drunk.

GRETE is sitting up again. Her make-up has run and she's very dishevelled.

Out of my way, he shouts, I have to get to my mum and her butcher, I have to examine her, to find out if he's had the old sow. Erna sits there as if struck by lightning, and Wottila's got such a look on his face, anyone would think he'd had another vision of the Virgin Mary. Herrmann sits down with a crash and shouts: Waiter... a barrel of beer, to flush the communion wafers down.

ERNA stands up making threatening gestures and moving towards MARIEDL. GRETE grabs ERNA and pushes her down in her chair again. GRETE holds ERNA there until ERNA hides her head in her apron.

GRETE: You need to keep sight of the truth as well, Erna. Life consumes whatever it wants. It can bring you a hard stool one day and a soft one the next. And whatever kind of stool life brings to you, well that's providence, and there's nothing you can do about it. So be a brave girl, and wait... till it's over. Go on, Mariedl.

MARIEDL: Wottila is the first one to pull himself together, and he says to Herrmann: How can you presume to speak in such a way of the woman who gave you the gift of life? Herrmann stands up, wipes his shoes on Wottila's suit, then empties a cup of milk coffee over Wottila's bald head. Wottila swiftly pulls his handkerchief from his trouser pocket and starts calmly doing battle with the coffee on his jacket. Then he says: May God forgive you, Herrmann, for what you do to him every second of your life. Each drop of blood from Christ's wounds only serves to flush you ever deeper into hell. And Herrmann says: What do you say to that, mum, what do you think about the way this exploiter of dead animals is speaking to your son? But Erna just squawks like a half-strangled goose. She probably isn't getting enough air, because it's so stuffy with all the spectators crowding round. But she still has just enough strength to spit in Herrmann's face. But Herrmann just falls about laughing. One pig spitting in another pig's face, he says, what difference does that make to anything. Then he calmly stands up, smooths back his hair, grabs Erna and Wottila by the scruffs of their necks, and bashes their heads together till the blood comes pouring out and their souls depart from this world. (*She breathes in deeply and stretches.*) And what of Mariedl standing there?

Mariedl stands there triumphant over all worldly things, with rays streaming out from between her legs. And the people's stool on her is all turning into gold dust. Meanwhile everyone's attacked Herrmann and tied him up and they keep on beating the scriptures into him with their fists till the police arrive. But Mariedl is floating up above the people, and everyone goes quiet, because they can see Mariedl's skin peeling off under the weight of the gold dust. She floats across to Erna and Wottila, who will be buried together, and strews a little bit of gold dust on their poor battered heads. Then the beautiful Mariedl floats over to poor Herrmann, who's never going to be let out of prison again, and bequeaths some gold dust to him as well. And Grete has to have some, because she's going straight to the loony bin, Hannelore has already fixed that up. And before Lore goes back to Australia, she too receives a sprinkle of gold from Mariedl.

Meanwhile ERNA and GRETE have stood up and are inspecting the kitchen knives on ERNA's sideboard. ERNA exits quietly to fetch a rag and bucket.

Mariedl's feet no longer know any pain, the floating is doing her good, also her feet are getting smaller and life is getting bigger and bigger. Even the priest doesn't look any bigger than a blowfly, because he's so far away. Up and up she floats. Lourdes is down there, it's the size of a matchbox. And there goes the Virgin Mary flying along. She has to go and appear to someone... she's hardly any bigger than a beetle. She looks very kind, the poor little thing.

Determinedly and very pragmatically, ERNA and GRETE approach MARIEDL. They carefully cut her throat all the way across. ERNA is ready with bucket and rag to prevent any excessive mess.

ERNA: Isn't it strange how a person smells from the inside. And why do people have so much blood in their flesh? I wouldn't be surprised if this one had a turd in her head as well. I'd really be interested to know.

GRETE: The tongue looks all right, I'll take that home for Lydi.

ERNA: Bright red blood, isn't it peaceful... you'd think everything would be going wild in someone who's just died.

GRETE: What shall we do with it?

ERNA: We'll bury her in the cellar, because everyone's got a body buried in their cellar, that's what they're always saying about this country.

Scene 3

The stage is a theatre. A small, grubby auditorium; a tiny stage framed in light bulbs. The "audience" sit on benches, backs to the real audience. During the performance, waitresses serve beer. The ORIGINAL BREECH-LOADING SOUL SOOTHERS are on stage. The "audience" shouts and yells.

LEAD SINGER: (*Of the ORIGINAL BREECH-LOADING SOUL SOOTHERS.*) And before the play, one last great song from the Original Breech-Loading Soul Soothers. This one's entitled "What I'd like the Lord to be for me".

Shouts and yells from the AUDIENCE.

If Jesus were an omnibus
I know He'd get me there
I'd climb up on that omnibus
And then I'd say my prayers

If Jesus were an omelette
How much He'd cost to make
You'd need a thousand eggs at least
And in your heart they'd break

If Jesus were a milk machine
The world would be His cow
Your heart is full of precious milk
And Jesus needs it now

If Jesus were an apple tree
His apples would be green
The sweet ones would be out of reach
And few and far between

If Jesus were a typewriter
You'd be the smallest key
So don't forget to taptaptap
Until your soul is free

Yes Jesus is the House of God
And you must be the heat
Be sure to keep your heart switched on
So you can warm His feet

Yes Jesus is a launderette
He'll wash you till you're clean
He'll wash away the dirty spots
Put your soul in His machine

A pressure cooker Jesus is
To cook you till you're soft
He'll cook your head until it's light
And send your soul aloft.

There's a noisy farewell to the ORIGINAL BREECH-LOADING SOUL SOOTHERS. The curtain falls then rises again. Three pretty young women are acting on the little stage, performing HOLY MOTHERS viciously, stridently, and with exaggeration. The "audience" laughs, and applauds at various points.

ERNA, GRETE and MARIEDL, sitting among the "audience", soon stand up horrified and try to leave. This is difficult because they are seated in the middle of a row. ERNA is the first to succeed in escaping and rattles one of the exit doors, which is closed. GRETE can't find an open door either. Only MARIEDL finds one. She rushes over to GRETE and drags her to the open door. GRETE frees herself, rushes to ERNA and drags her to the open door as well. All three disappear. HOLY MOTHERS continues on the stage for a while.

The End.